Tell About Toys

by Aimee Louise
photos by Sonny Senser

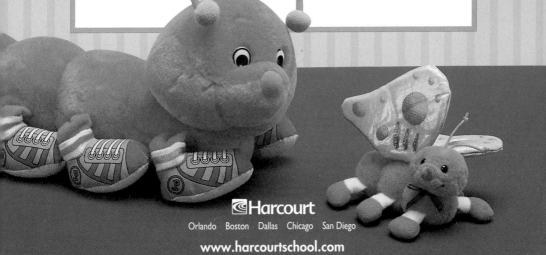

Harcourt

Orlando Boston Dallas Chicago San Diego

www.harcourtschool.com

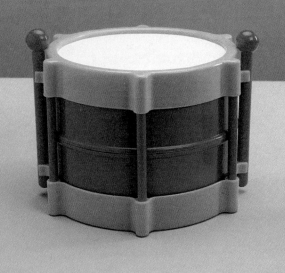

large

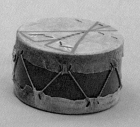

small

2

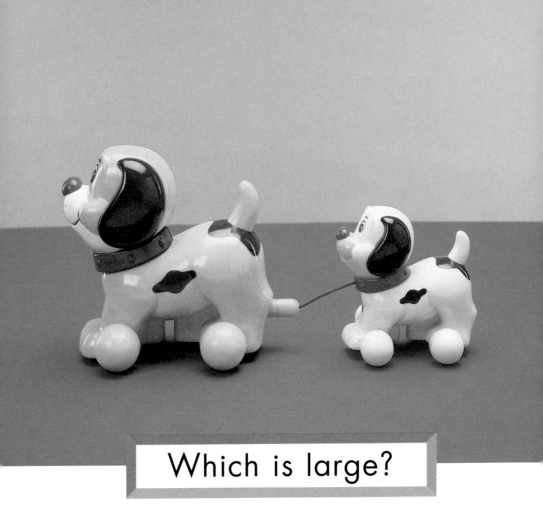

Which is large?

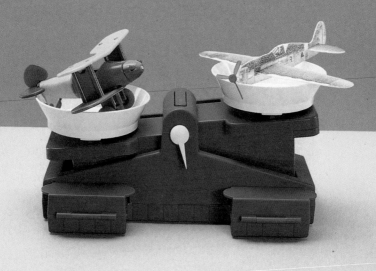

heavy   light

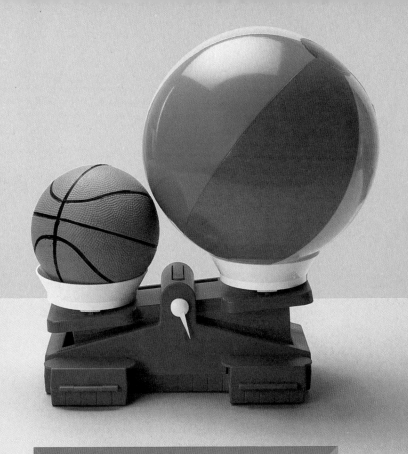

Which is heavy?

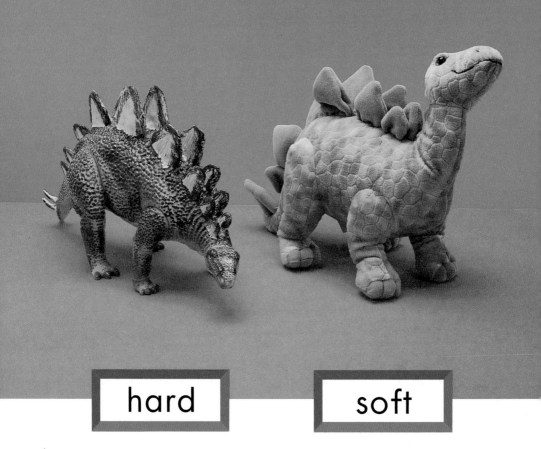

hard   soft

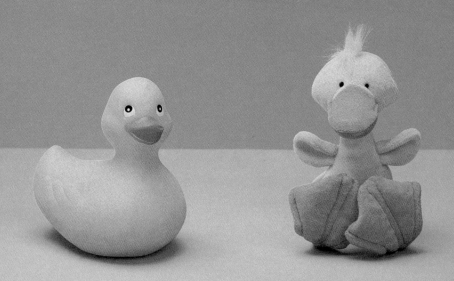

Which is soft?

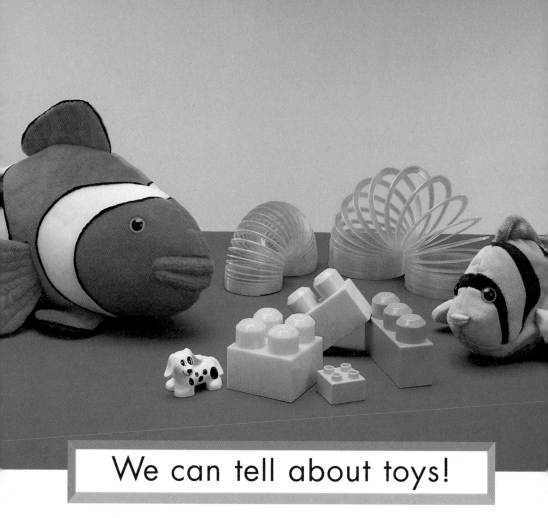

We can tell about toys!